MW01129923

Third Position
Preparatory studies

for the cello

by Cassia Harvey

CHP296

www.charveypublications.com - print books
www.learnstrings.com - PDF downloadable books
www.harveystringarrangements.com - chamber music

Study Notes

1. Keep each finger curved as you shift with it.

2. Stay in each position until a finger number tells you to shift to a new position.

3. **Finger charts** for the third position notes that are studied in this volume are located at the back of the book.

1. Shifting to D from 1st Finger

Cassia Harvey

Down Home

Trad., arr. Harvey

2. Shifting to D in Arpeggios

Cowboy's Lament

Trad., arr. Harvey

3. Shifting to D and Testing with Open D

Star Music

Harvey

4. Learning 3rd Finger E

German Folk Tune

Trad., arr. Harvey

5. Playing 3rd Finger E

Fisherman's Chantey

Trad., arr. Harvey

6. 3rd Finger Exercise

Variation on "The Campbells are Coming"

Trad., arr. Harvey

7. Learning 4th Finger F

The Young Lady

Trad., arr. Harvey

8. Playing 4th Finger F

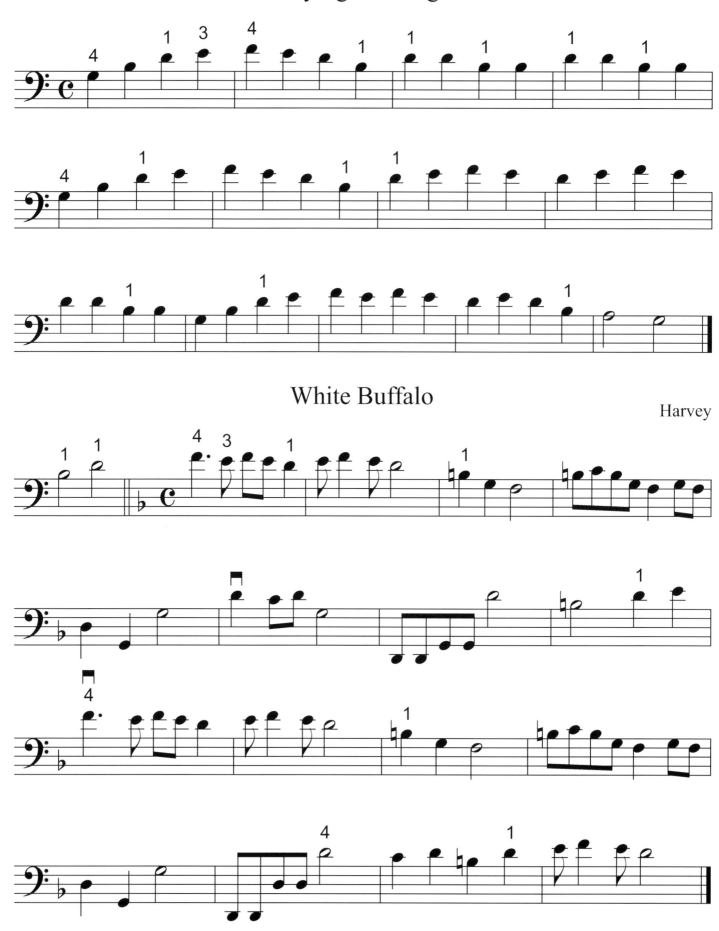

White Buffalo

Harvey

9. 4th Finger Study

Fiddler's Fancy

Harvey

10. Finger Exercise with 4th Finger

April Rainstorm

Harvey

11. Skipping from 1st to 4th Finger

Pretty Peggy

Trad., arr. Harvey

12. Shifting to D from 2nd Fingers

Russian Vespers

Trad., arr. Harvey

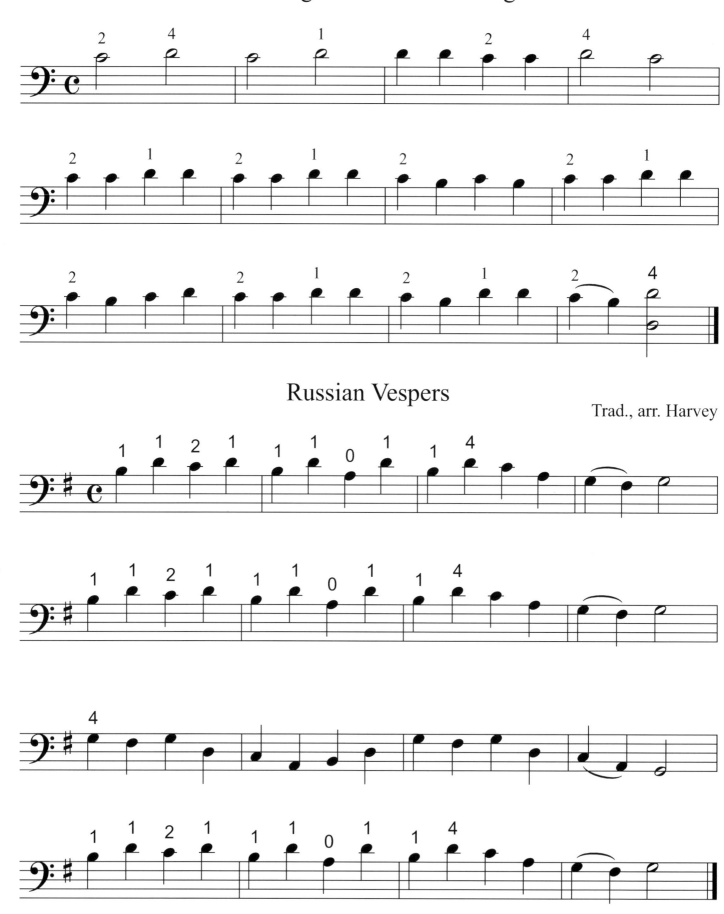

13. Shifting from 2nd Finger and Playing E

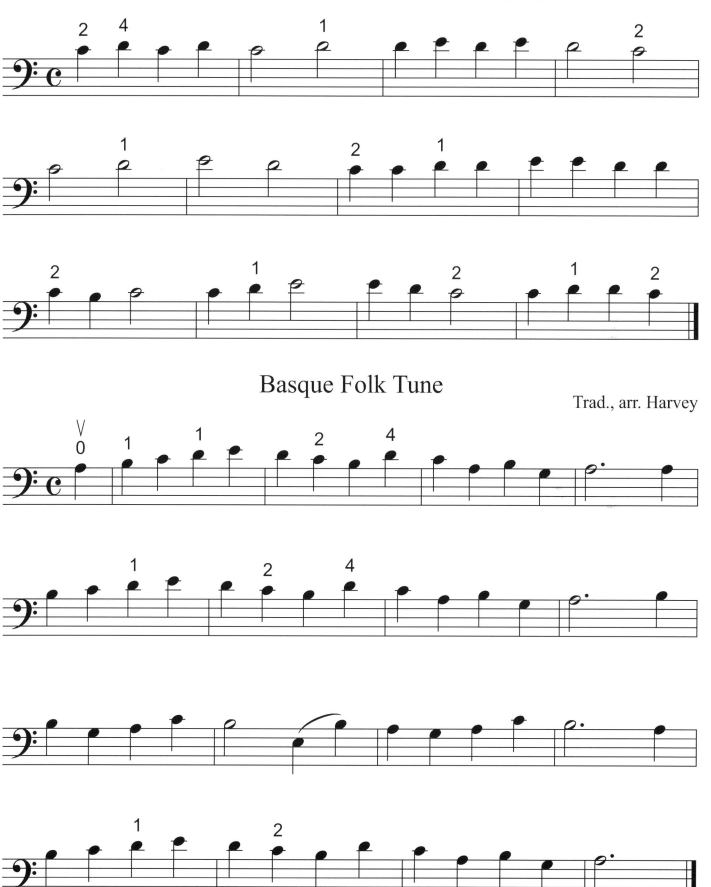

Basque Folk Tune

Trad., arr. Harvey

14. Shifting from 2nd Finger and Playing F

By Our Gates

Trad., arr. Harvey

15. More Shifting from 2nd Finger

Johnny's Gone for a Soldier

Trad., arr. Harvey

16. Skipping from 1st to 4th Finger

Sarasponda

Trad., arr. Harvey

17. Shifting to D from 1st and 2nd Fingers

March

Bach, arr. Harvey

18. Shifting to D from 3rd Finger

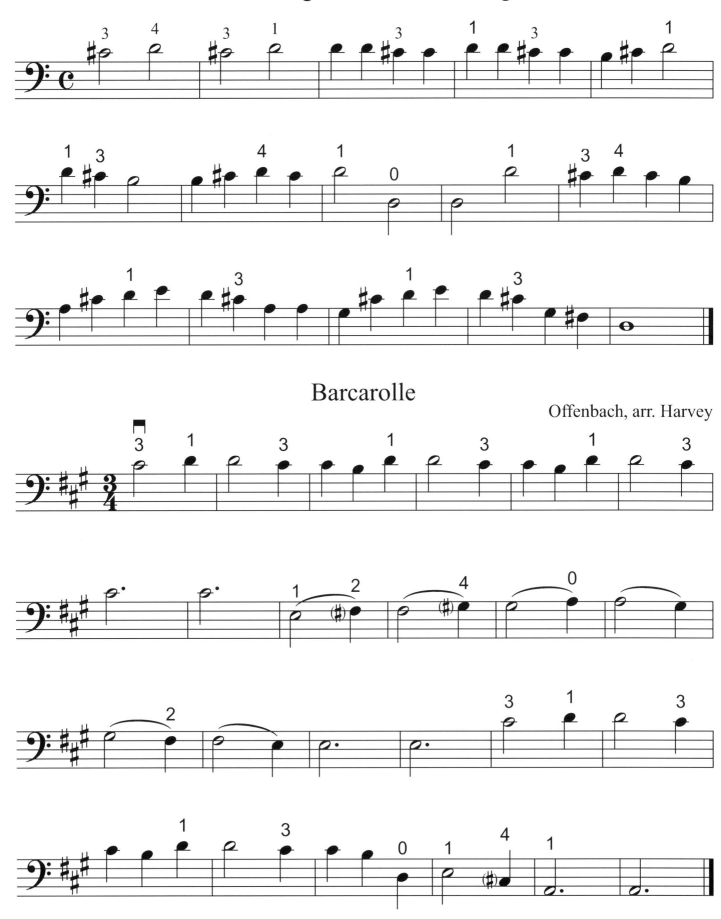

Barcarolle

Offenbach, arr. Harvey

19. 3rd Finger Shifting Etude

Fum, Fum, Fum

Trad., arr. Harvey

20. 3rd Finger Study

Mineral Springs

Harvey

21. Shifting to D from 4th Finger

Cerulean Waltz

Harvey

22. 3rd Position Study

Zum Gali

Trad., arr. Harvey

Fine

D. C. al Fine

23. 3rd Position Rhythm Study

Liza Jane

Trad., arr. Harvey

24. 3rd Position Finger Exercise

The County Squire

Harvey

25. Shifting to G from 1st Finger

Castle Kelly

Trad., arr. Harvey

26. Shifting to G from 1st Finger

Chinese Folk Tune

Trad., arr. Harvey

27. Stretching to 2nd Finger A

Extend 2nd finger ↑
to play A.

Lullaby

Harvey

28. More Stretching to 2nd Finger A

Camptown Races

Foster, arr. Harvey

29. Shifting and Stretching Study

The Tired Banjo

Harvey

30. Learning 4th Finger B

The Last Bohemian

Harvey

31. Stretching in 3rd Position

The Empty Prairie

Harvey

32. Checking First Finger Intonation

Wayfaring Stranger

Trad., arr. Harvey

33. Stretching Study

There's a Hole in the Bucket, Dear Liza

Trad., arr. Harvey

34. Stretching Finger Exercise

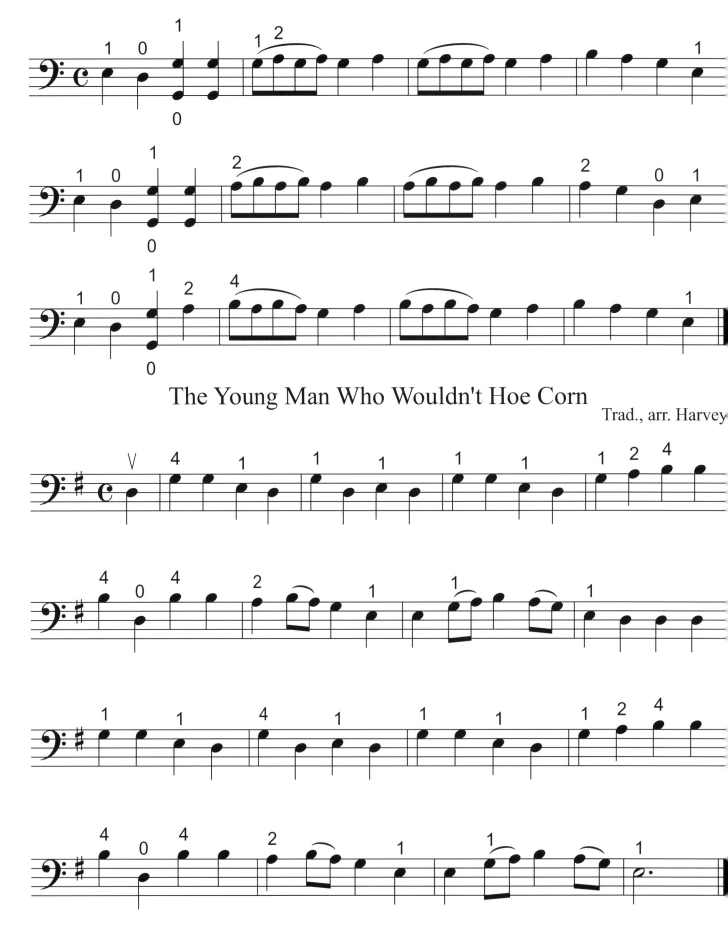

The Young Man Who Wouldn't Hoe Corn

Trad., arr. Harvey

35. Stretching Study

Woven Coverlet

Harvey

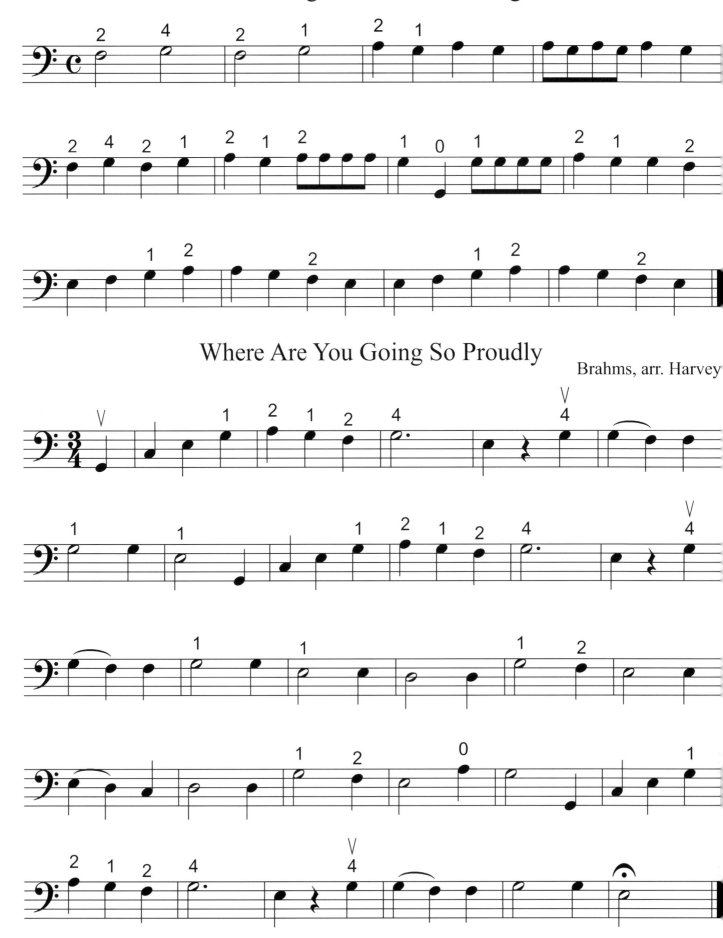

36. Shifting to G from 2nd Finger

Where Are You Going So Proudly

Brahms, arr. Harvey

37. Shifting in Scale Patterns

Irish Lament

Harvey

38. Testing 1st Finger with Open G

Erie Canal

Trad., arr. Harvey

39. Stretching Between 4th and 1st Fingers

Old Hob

Walsh, arr. Harvey

40. Shifting to G from F♯

The Farmer Comes to Town

Trad., arr. Harvey

41. Shifting from 3rd Finger and Stretching

Sailing for San Francisco

Trad., arr. Harvey

42. Stretching Between 1st and 4th Finger

Turkish March

Trad., arr. Harvey

43. Shifting to G from 4th Finger

Old Tare River

Trad., arr. Harvey

44. Third Position Study

Landler

Harvey

45. F Major Scales

46. Square Dance

Trad., arr. Harvey

A String

First Position

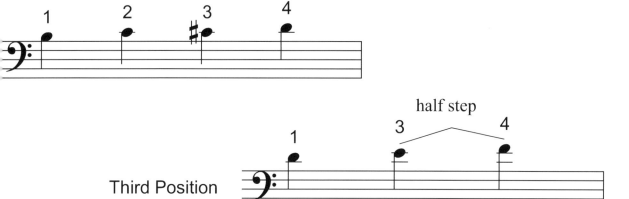

Third Position

half step

D   E   F

D string

First Position

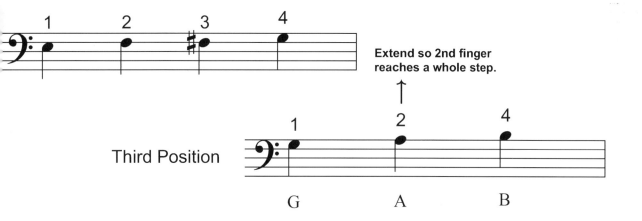

Extend so 2nd finger
reaches a whole step.

Third Position

G   A   B

Preparatory Exercises for Movement One

1. Fourth Position Notes and Bowing
Measures 1-3

Now the key signature changes, so the rest of this exercise will use 3rd finger F♯ in 4th position.

Match the sound of the 4th finger to the open string.

Made in United States
Orlando, FL
26 June 2022

19169850R00028